THE

Golfer's

COMPANION

THE ESSENTIAL AUSTRALIAN GUIDE
TO GOLF RULES, COMPETITIONS,
SCORING AND BETTING GAMES

Damien Davis & Scott Blackman

The Golfer's Companion

The Essential Australian Guide to Golf Rules, Competitions, Scoring and Betting Games

Ironbark
Pan Macmillan Australia

Dedicated to my lovely wife Tara, my Mum and Dad, and my mentor and friend Damien
SCOTT BLACKMAN

Dedicated to the members of Team Besity (Stork, PK, Winsey, Ackers, Blackie, Harps, Macka, Hibbo, Phil, Shep and Knighty), and to the Blackman family for arranging my membership to the magnificent Riversdale Golf Club
DAMIEN DAVIS

First published in 1999 in Ironbark by Pan Macmillan Australia Pty Limited
St Martins Tower, 31 Market Street, Sydney

National Library of Australia
cataloguing-in-publication data:

Davis, Damien.
The golfer's companion.

ISBN 0 330 36202 X.

Golf. I. Blackman, Scott. II. Title.

796.352

Designed by Kerry Klinner
Set in Garamond 10/12 pt
Printed in Australia by McPherson's Printing Group

CONTENTS

INTRODUCTION

Golf is a great game played in superb surroundings and usually with good friends. Golf is full of highs, like chipping in or smashing a drive that bisects the fairway; and lows, like four-putting from 15 feet or taking three shots in a bunker. If, as many golfers do, you only ever score by counting your strokes, then the lows can destroy your round.

The Golfer's Companion is about all the different types of golf competition that give you new challenges and new methods of scoring, and rekindle your enthusiasm when stroke-counting has become boring. To these new competitions you can add in the extra pizzazz of having a side game amongst friends.

So if you always wanted to know what all the numbers on a scorecard really mean, how Stableford points are scored, how Canadian Foursomes works, why some opponents hiss when you take a long second putt, how to score in split sixes or why the person next to you at the clubhouse bar won five dollars for a Sandy, find out by reading this book. In addition, to solve any arguments that might arise out on the course or to save you any embarrassment, *The Golfer's Companion* also includes a simplified explanation of the major golf rules and golfing etiquette. Take this book with you in your golf bag as a ready reckoner.

Remember, golf is there to be enjoyed, so maintain some variety through scoring and some challenge through your betting.

SIMPLIFIED RULES AND ETIQUETTE

The Royal and Ancient Golf Club of St Andrews (R&A) Rules of Golf are the definitive guide as to what is — and is not — permissible in golf. The R&A rules book is available from most golf clubs and all State Golf Association offices, or players can access rules information via the Australian Golf Union (AGU) website: www.agu.org.au. However, this simplified guide should improve your knowledge of the etiquette and rules, and provide you with a quick reference source before, during and after a round.

The easiest way to get to know the rules (R) and etiquette (E) of golf is to divide them up into the following:

- Before you tee-off
- On the tee
- On the fairway/In the rough
- In bunkers or hazards
- On the green
- After nine holes
- After eighteen holes.

Before you tee-off

- You must dress according to the standards set by the club. At any club you are safe if you wear a plain polo shirt, slacks and golf shoes. (E)
- You are not allowed to carry more than 14 clubs in your bag — even if you can afford more. (R)
- Most clubs either recommend or insist that you wear golf shoes, preferably without metal spikes, to avoid damaging the course. (E)
- Most clubs either recommend or insist that your buggy is fitted with slicks (fat wheels), particularly in winter. (E)
- With your playing partners, decide on the type of competition you're going to play and/or the method of betting (make sure you are clear about the stakes). (E)
- Check in at the Pro Shop to pay green fees and pay competition fees, pick up a scorecard, check on local rules or reserve a tee-off time. (E)
- If you are playing in a club competition make sure you know which competition it is, ie, Par, Stableford, etc. (R)
- Collect a sand bucket to carry with you on the course to fill divots. (E)

On the tee

- Mark your card with your name, club, handicap, etc and swap cards with your marker (ie, the playing partner who will fill in your score) for the round. (E)
- Check the number and brand of your ball and put an identification mark on it to make sure it is different to your playing partners'. (R)
- Warm-up practice swings should be made away from the tee-off area. (E)
- The first player to tee-off has the honour. On the first hole, players tee-off in order of lowest to highest handicap, or by the toss of a coin. On subsequent holes, the order of tee-off is from lowest to highest score according to the previous hole. (R)
- You should never talk or move whilst a player is about to tee-off. (E)
- You should stand a safe distance behind the player teeing off and watch where the ball goes. (E)
- You should never tee-off until the group in front is out of range, which usually means they have left the green on a Par 3, or have all played their second shots and are moving to play their third on a Par 4 or 5 hole. (E)
- If your tee shot is heading towards another player, or where you suspect there might be other players, you must immediately yell 'fore'. (E)

- Once you address your ball (take your stance ready to hit it), any fresh-air swing counts as a stroke. (R)
- You must not tee-off in front of, outside, or more than two club lengths behind, the tee markers. (R)
- Generally, white tee markers are for men, red are for women and other colours are for visitors/green fee payers. (E)
- You should replace or fill divot holes with sand or your divot, depending on the course requirements. (E)
- If your tee shot is wayward and heads off into deep bush (lost ball territory), near water or over boundary fences (out of bounds), you should immediately play a provisional ball from the tee just in case you cannot find, or play, your original ball. Your provisional tee-off counts as your third stroke (one for the original shot, one stroke penalty and one for the provisional shot). (R)

ON THE FAIRWAY/IN THE ROUGH

- You should never talk or move whilst a player is taking a shot. (E)
- You should call 'fore' if your shot is heading towards another player. (E)
- You should never hit until the group in front is out of range, which usually means they have left the green on a Par 4, or all players have played their third shot onto the green on a Par 5. (E)
- You should play your shots without delay and walk quickly between shots. (E)
- On the fairway, the player who is furthest from the hole plays first and all playing partners should stand behind the ball (not nearer to the hole) of that player. If your ball has stopped in someone else's divot hole, you must play it from where it lies, but if your ball is plugged (buried) in the fairway, you may lift it out, clean it, and drop it close to the same spot but no nearer the hole. (R)
- You should replace or fill all divots with sand. (E)
- If you hear someone call 'fore' cover your head. (E)
- If your tee shot or fairway shot is lost, out of bounds (OOB) or unplayable, you can continue to play your provisional ball. However, if you did not play a provisional ball after your wayward shot, then you must go back and drop another ball as near as possible to the spot from which your original ball was played and take a one-stroke penalty. In the case of an unplayable

ball, you can also opt to drop another ball within two club lengths of the unplayable spot and take a penalty stroke. (R)

- You should not look for a lost ball for more than five minutes. The ball is deemed lost if it is not found within five minutes. (R)
- If your ball lands on a section of the course marked with a GUR (ground under repair) sign, or in a rabbit scrape, or in casual (temporary) water such as a puddle, you may retrieve your ball and drop it within one club length of the nearest point of relief, without penalty, outside the above areas but no nearer to the hole. (R)
- If your ball lies in long grass, in reeds, under bushes or amongst fallen leaves and sticks, you may only remove loose impediments such as sticks, leaves and stones provided the ball does not move. If the ball does move you get a one-stroke penalty and the ball must be replaced. You must not improve the ball's lie by stamping down grass or breaking off branches. If you do, you will receive a two-stroke penalty in Stroke Play and loss of hole in Match Play. (R)
- If your ball comes to rest next to an immovable obstruction such as a sprinkler, drink fountain or sand barrel, you may lift and drop your ball without penalty within one club length of the nearest point of relief and no nearer the hole. (R)
- If your stance or swing are impeded by a staked tree, you may lift and drop your ball no nearer the hole with no penalty. (R)

In bunkers or hazards

- If your ball lands in a water hazard (sea, lake, pond, river, ditch) marked with yellow stakes, you can play it without penalty. If you choose not to play it, you must take a one-stroke penalty and either play a new ball from the spot where you played your original ball, or drop another ball behind the hazard in line with where it entered the hazard. (R)
- If your ball lands in a lateral water hazard marked by red stakes, you can choose to play it. If you choose not to play it, you must drop another ball within two club lengths of where your original ball entered the hazard and take a one-stroke penalty. (R)
- In any hazard, you must not take practice swings in which you ground your club (touch the ground). If you do, you receive a two-stroke penalty in Stroke Play or loss of the hole in Match Play. (R)
- Rakes in bunkers are considered to be moveable obstructions and can be removed without penalty if impeding your shot in a bunker. If your ball moves when you remove the rake, place it back on the original spot. (R)
- You must rake smooth footprints and explosion craters after playing a bunker shot. (E)

ON THE GREEN

- The furthest player from the hole putts first. (R)
- You may mark your ball and clean it prior to putting. (R)
- You may remove sand, soil, leaves or stones in line between your ball and the hole. (R)
- You should repair pitch marks (dints) made by balls landing on the green, but you must not repair shoe-spike marks until after you have putted out. (R)
- You should not step on any playing partner's line to the hole. (E)
- If you are putting or chipping/pitching from off the green, the flag may remain in the hole. There is no penalty if the ball hits the flag. (R)
- If a playing partner's ball is blocking your line to the hole or is in such a position that your ball may collide with it, have your partner mark his/her ball. (R)
- When you are on the green you may have the flag removed, attended (held) or held over the hole to assist your putting, but your putt must not hit the flag or the person holding it. You will receive a two-stroke penalty if it does. (R)
- When you have completed the hole, mark your scorecard before teeing-off on the next hole but do not stand on the green to mark your card. (E)

After nine holes

- You are permitted to have a quick drink or snack at the clubhouse but do not take more than five minutes. (E)
- Check the scores for each hole and tally up the nine-hole totals. (E)

After eighteen holes

- Quickly move away from the 18th green. (E)
- Check the scores for each hole and tally up the 18-hole totals. (R)
- Sign the cards as player/marker. (R)
- Make sure your handicap is recorded on the card. (R)
- Hand in your card at the Pro Shop or place it in the correct box if you are in a competition or wish the card to be passed on to the handicapper. (E)

All State Golf Associations conduct rules education courses and all regular golfers are advised to contact their Association for further details.

YOUR HANDICAP

Whilst you may think that your handicap is your atrocious putting or your wicked slice, handicaps are in fact carefully calculated ratings that aim to even out competition. Rather than the best golfer thrashing the field every round, when handicaps are used every player has a chance to win and to keep the good golfers constantly challenged.

HOW TO GET A HANDICAP

The Australian Golf Handicapping System was developed by the Australian Golf Union (AGU) and is administered Australia-wide by the AGU and Womens Golf Australia, to ensure uniformity of golf handicaps.

The Australian Golf Handicap is a numerical figure which reflects a golfer's ability. Good golfers have lower handicaps and less talented golfers higher handicaps. Handicaps allow golfers of different abilities to compete against one another with each golfer having a fair chance of winning.

To understand how handicaps are calculated you need to know two terms:

Par for the course: A regulation number of strokes are allocated for each hole, eg par 3, par 4, par 5 and par for the course is the total par for the 18 holes.

Australian Course Rating (ACR): The ACR is a figure given to each golf course to allow comparisons between courses. The figure is allocated by the Golf Association in each State and takes into account the length of the course and the difficulty of the holes. For example two different courses may have identical pars of 72, however, on one course all the holes may be longer, all the fairways tree- or water-lined and all the greens surrounded by bunkers. In this case the ACR for the easy course may be 70 or below and for the difficult course 73 or higher.

After each competition round the ACR is adjusted according to the scores returned by all competitors. The new figure is called the Calculated Course Rating (CCR).

All golf clubs have a designated club member who calculates members' initial handicaps and then adjusts them as required. Adjustment of handicaps for club members will soon be controlled by a centralised national computer system developed by the AGU, called Golflink. Basically, your handicap is the average number of strokes you take above the CCR for the course. For example, if the CCR for the course is 72 and you regularly go around in 96, then your handicap is 24.

To earn a handicap you must submit five 18-hole cards, from which the handicapper determines your handicap. Of course, for handicapping to

Player(s) Damien Davis FOR

Home Club Riversdale HANDICAP

MENS				PLAYER			MARKER			LADIES			
HOLE	METRES	PAR	RATING		+ − 0			+ − 0		MATCH	PAR /STAB.	PAR	METRES
1	195	3	3/30	4						17	12	3	150
2	350	4	5/24	5						9	1	4	306
3	344	4	12/29	4						13	12	4	272
4	154	3	13	4						7	6	3	135
5	392	4	1/20	5						15	17	5	386
6	495	5	15/25	6						5	8	5	442
7	362	4	7/27	5						3	3	4	345
8	476	5	11/22	5						1	5	5	428
9	312	4	9	5						11	10	4	300
OUT	3080	36		43								37	2764

Player D Davis

Marker

Date 15/9/99

PLEASE REPAIR DIVOTS WITH SAND

Figure 1: Scorecard adjusted to calculate handicap

HANDICAP

COURSE	✓	A.C.R.	A.L.C.R.	C.C.R.	SCORE
MENS		71			
LADIES			73		

MENS				PLAYER			MARKER			LADIES			
HOLE	METRES	PAR	RATING		+ − 0			+ − 0		MATCH	PAR /STAB.	PAR	METRES
10	237	4	18	5						18	18	4	225
11	510	5	14/26	~~8~~	7					4	7	5	482
12	281	4	16/32	5						10	9	4	256
13	355	4	2/21	6						2	2	4	322
14	147	3	10/31	4						16	16	3	110
15	532	5	6/19	7						8	11	5	391
16	395	4	4/23	6						6	4	4	360
17	190	3	8/28	3						12	13	3	148
18	281	4	17	5						14	15	4	239
IN	2928	36		~~49~~	48							36	2533
OUT	3080	36		43								37	2764
TOT	6008	72		~~92~~	91							73	5297
DEDUCT HANDICAP										ENTRY NO.			
NET TOTAL													

REPAIR BALL MARKS

work, it is presumed that all players submit honest cards for handicapping. The maximum Australian handicap for males is 27 and for females 45. Club handicaps above these figures may be allocated by your club.

If you are not a club member, then you can calculate your own handicap amongst your regular golf friends. To calculate your handicap, the maximum number of strokes allowed on any hole is a double bogey (two over par), so adjust your scorecard accordingly. For example, an adjusted round of 91 is 20 strokes over the ACR, so you would have a handicap of 20 (see Figure 1). Next, average your handicap for your last five rounds. For example, adjusted rounds of 91, 93, 87, 93 and 91 would give you handicaps of 20, 22, 16, 22 and 20, which averages out to a handicap of 20.

The Callaway handicap system

The Callaway handicap system, invented and copyrighted by golf professional Lionel F. Callaway in 1957, is used to determine fair handicaps when a group of novice, occasional or unhandicapped regular golfers get together to play a competition. In this system, each player's handicap is worked out after the round so the player will not know his or her handicap until after completion of the 18th hole.

SCORE					DEDUCT
68	69	70	71	72	Scratch – no adjustment
73	74	75			½ worst hole and adjustment
76	77	78	79	80	1 worst hole and adjustment
81	82	83	84	85	1½ worst holes and adjustment
86	87	88	89	90	2 worst holes and adjustment
91	92	93	94	95	2½ worst holes and adjustment
96	97	98	99	100	3 worst holes and adjustment
101	102	103	104	105	3½ worst holes and adjustment
106	107	108	109	110	4 worst holes and adjustment
111	112	113	114	115	4½ worst holes and adjustment
116	117	118	119	120	5 worst holes and adjustment
121	122	123	124	125	5½ worst holes and adjustment
126	127	128	129	130	6 worst holes and adjustment
				ADJUSTMENT	
–2	–1	0	+1	+2	Add to or deduct from handicap

Figure 2: The Callaway Adjustment Table

To calculate each player's handicap, deduct from their gross score for 18 holes their scores on several of their worst holes according to the table in Figure 2. For example, if a player's gross score for 18 holes is 109, he or she may deduct their four worst holes according to the following rules:

- The maximum score allowed on any hole is twice its par.

Player(s) *Luke Davis*

Home Club *—*

MENS				PLAYER			MARKER			LADIES			
HOLE	METRES	PAR	RATING		+10			+10		MATCH	PAR /STAB.	PAR	METRES
1	195	3	3/30	*6*						17	12	3	150
2	350	4	5/24	*(8)*						9	1	4	306
3	344	4	12/29	*6*						13	12	4	272
4	154	3	13	*5*						7	6	3	135
5	392	4	1/20	*(8)*						15	17	5	386
6	495	5	15/25	*7*						5	8	5	442
7	362	4	7/27	*6*						3	3	4	345
8	476	5	11/22	*7*						1	5	5	428
9	312	4	9	*6*						11	10	4	300
OUT	3080	36		*59*								37	2764

Player *L. Davis*

Marker *LM*

Date *11/4/99*

PLEASE REPAIR DIVOTS WITH SAND

Figure 3: A sample scorecard adjusted using the Callaway handicap system

HANDICAP
33

COURSE	✓	A.C.R.	A.L.C.R.	C.C.R.	SCORE
MENS		71			76
LADIES			73		

MENS				PLAYER			MARKER			LADIES			
HOLE	METRES	PAR	RATING		+ − 0			+ − 0		MATCH	PAR/STAB.	PAR	METRES
10	237	4	18	4						18	18	4	225
11	510	5	14/26	6						4	7	5	482
12	281	4	16/32	5						10	9	4	256
13	355	4	2/21	~~9~~	(8)					2	2	4	322
14	147	3	10/31	4						16	16	3	110
15	532	5	6/19	(8)						8	11	5	391
16	395	4	4/23	5						6	4	4	360
17	190	3	8/28	4						12	13	3	148
18	281	4	17	5						14	15	4	239
IN	2928	36		50								36	2533
OUT	3080	36		59								37	2764
TOT	6008	72		109								73	5297
DEDUCT HANDICAP										ENTRY NO.			
NET TOTAL													

REPAIR BALL MARKS

- Scores on the 17th and 18th holes are never deducted.

Figure 3 shows a sample scorecard. The player's gross score is 109, but on the 13th hole, he shot a nine and the maximum allowable is an eight (twice par). So the four worst holes out of holes one to 16 are the 2nd, 5th, 13th and 15th with scores of 8, 8, 8 (adjusted) and 8, which adds up to 32. According to Figure 2, a gross score of 109 requires a +1 adjustment to the handicap, so the final handicap is 33. Therefore, our sample player, Luke Davis, has a final net score of 109 – 33 = 76.

In performing the calculations for the Callaway handicap, half strokes are rounded up. For example, 10½ becomes 11 and if two players tie on the final score, the player with the lowest handicap is the winner.

With the Callaway handicap system, a few bad holes will not destroy a player's round because these are the ones generally deducted from the score. As a result, players can afford to take some chances and play aggressively, particularly if they have scored well early in the round.

THE SCORECARD

Before launching into the many types of golf competitions you must be familiar with the scorecard. Scorecards vary slightly from club to club, but there are a number of features common to all scorecards. All scorecards provide you with certain information, which we'll call 'information given', and all scorecards require you to record certain information, which we'll call 'information added'.

INFORMATION GIVEN

As you can see in Figures 4 and 5, the information given to you by the scorecard includes:

- The local rules for each golf course. These are usually on the back of the card and include important information about out of bounds (OOB), ground under repair (GUR), hazards, staked trees, buildings or equipment, power lines and watering systems. Read this before you start your round so you know what to avoid and where you can take a drop without penalty (see Figure 5) and the location of distance markers.
- The back of the card often includes a map of the course layout.
- Each hole numbered 1–18 with the distance in

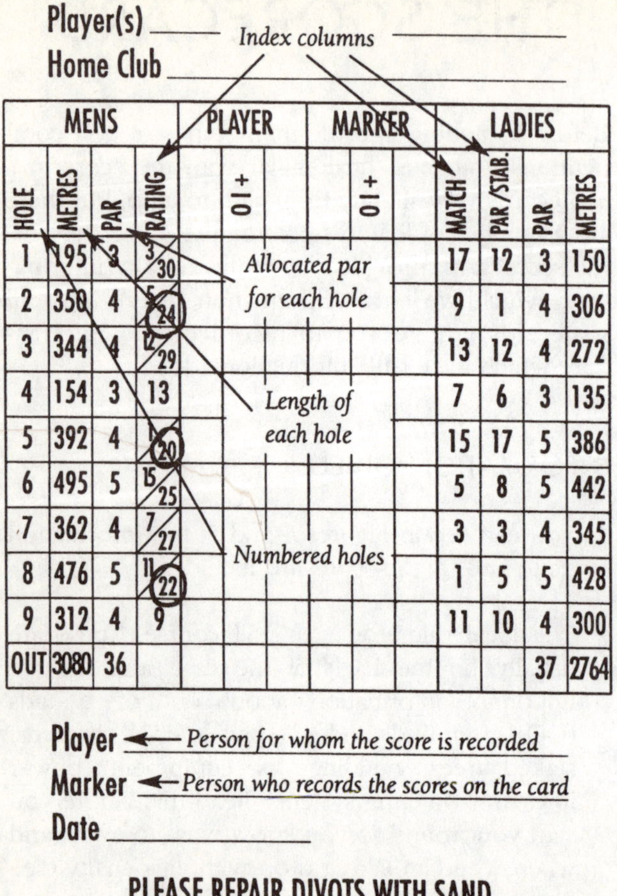

MENS				PLAYER			MARKER			LADIES			
HOLE	METRES	PAR	RATING		+10			+10		MATCH	PAR /STAB.	PAR	METRES
1	195	3	3 / 30							17	12	3	150
2	350	4	5 / 24							9	1	4	306
3	344	4	12 / 29							13	12	4	272
4	154	3	13							7	6	3	135
5	392	4	1 / 20							15	17	5	386
6	495	5	15 / 25							5	8	5	442
7	362	4	7 / 27							3	3	4	345
8	476	5	11 / 22							1	5	5	428
9	312	4	9							11	10	4	300
OUT	3080	36										37	2764

Figure 4: A sample scorecard

HANDICAP
24

COURSE	✓	A.C.R.	A.L.C.R.	C.C.R.	SCORE
MENS		71			
LADIES			73		

MENS				PLAYER			MARKER			LADIES			
HOLE	METRES	PAR	RATING		+10			+10		MATCH	PAR /STAB.	PAR	METRES
10	237	4	18							18	18	4	225
11	510	5	14/26							4	7	5	482
12	281	4	16/32							10	9	4	256
13	355	4	2/21							2	2	4	322
14	147	3	10/31							16	16	3	110
15	532	5	6/19							8	11	5	391
16	395	4	4/23							6	4	4	360
17	190	3	8/28							12	13	3	148
18	281	4	17							14	15	4	239
IN	2928	36										36	2533
OUT	3080	36										37	2764
TOT	6008	72										73	5297
DEDUCT HANDICAP										ENTRY NO.			
NET TOTAL													

REPAIR BALL MARKS

metres for both men and women.

- The par (allocated number of strokes) for each hole along with the total par for each nine holes (out: holes 1–9; in: holes 10–18) and the total par for the course.
- The ACR for the course.
- One or more index columns. An index column rates the degree of difficulty of each hole, with the hole rated 1 being the hardest to play, and 18 being the easiest hole. For example, in Figure 4, for men the fifth hole is considered the hardest while the tenth is considered the easiest.

Some clubs choose to have two separate index columns (see Figure 4, ladies), one for Stroke Play which includes Par, Stableford and Four Ball competitions and one for Match Play. Therefore in Stroke Play competition you use the Stroke/Par/Stableford index and in Match Play the Match index.

The significance of index columns is that they show you where you receive strokes, depending on your handicap. For example, if you have a 24 handicap you will receive a one-stroke deduction on every hole and a second stroke deduction on the six hardest holes rated 1–6. However, some golf courses give two strokes in a different order.

For example, in Figure 4, a 24-handicapper would receive two strokes on holes indexed 19 to 24 (which are holes 2, 5, 8, 13, 15 and 16) and one stroke on all other holes.

LOCAL RULES

1. "OUT OF BOUNDS"

(a) All ground beyond the Club's boundary fences.

2. "WATER HAZARDS"

(a) Areas defined within yellow stakes are Water Hazards.

(b) Areas defined within red stakes are Lateral Water Hazards.

(c) Relief from water hazards behind greens may be taken by dropping a ball under penalty of one stroke in the nearest dropping zone.

3. "GARDENS"

Garden beds (as defined on the Notice Board) shall be treated as G.U.R. Play prohibited. The player MUST take relief under Rule 25-1.

4. "GROUND UNDER REPAIR"

GROUND UNDER REPAIR includes garden beds, all areas defined by white stakes or lines, and motorised wheel marks. Relief must be taken as provided in Rule 25-1.

5. "STAKED TREES"

If a staked tree interferes with the player's stance or area of intended swing, the ball must be lifted, without penalty, and dropped in accordance with the procedure prescribed under Rule 24-2b(1) (immovable obstruction).

NOTE

Stakes or wire protecting young trees are immovable obstructions.

6. "WATER EROSION IN BUNKERS"

In bunkers, areas eroded by water may be treated as G.U.R. and relief taken as provided in rule 25-1.

7. "FIXED SPRINKLER HEADS/TAP COVERS/GRATES"

Specimen Local Rule No 1, Part B, Appendix 1 of the Rules of Golf applies.

8. "DRAINS"

Through the green, all drains are integral parts of the course.

PENALTY FOR BREACH OF LOCAL RULE

Match Play: Loss of Hole. Stroke Play: Two Strokes.

Note 1. DISTANCE MARKERS on the Sprinkler Heads show metres to the centre of the green.

Note 2. See notice boards for definition of practice areas and garden beds.

Note 3. Grassed slopes of Bunkers are not closely mown areas – Rule 25-2 does not apply.

SAND BUCKETS MUST BE CARRIED AND USED

Figure 5: **Sample scorecard — local rules**

INFORMATION ADDED

The information you add to the scorecard must be accurate and should include:

- The player's name, score, handicap and his or her signature at the end of the round. Remember, you are 'the marker' and you score for someone else: 'the player'. You never score for yourself.
- Your score, signature and date as the marker (see Figure 6). After you complete the card as marker, you hand it back to the player to sign.

INDIVIDUAL COMPETITIONS

STROKE

Stroke is the original and most common type of golf competition. In a Stroke competition, the number of strokes taken at each hole is entered on each player's card then totalled for each nine holes and the full 18 holes (see Figure 6). If players are using handicaps, then each player's handicap is deducted from his or her gross (total) score to give a net result, which is used to determine competition results. The player with the lowest net score is the winner.

Stroke is considered to be the true test of a golfer's ability, which is why it is used in professional tournaments. To win Stroke competitions you must be consistent, because one bad hole usually eliminates your chances of winning. So when you play Stroke, do not go for 'hero' shots, instead play percentage (or safe) golf.

Player(s) Emma Davis

Home Club —

MENS				PLAYER			MARKER			LADIES			
HOLE	METRES	PAR	RATING		+ – 0			+ – 0		MATCH	PAR /STAB.	PAR	METRES
1	195	3	3/30	7			4			17	12	3	150
2	350	4	5/24	6			6			9	1	4	306
3	344	4	12/29	4			3			13	12	4	272
4	154	3	13	4			4			7	6	3	135
5	392	4	1/20	6			5			15	17	5	386
6	495	5	15/25	7			7			5	8	5	442
7	362	4	7/27	6			5			3	3	4	345
8	476	5	11/22	5			5			1	5	5	428
9	312	4	9	4			3			11	10	4	300
OUT	3080	36		49			42					37	2764

Player E. Davis

Marker [signature]

Date 1/4/99

PLEASE REPAIR DIVOTS WITH SAND

Figure 6: Individual Stroke competition

HANDICAP
30

COURSE	✓	A.C.R.	A.L.C.R.	C.C.R.	SCORE
MENS		71			66
LADIES			73		

MENS				PLAYER			MARKER			LADIES			
HOLE	METRES	PAR	RATING		+10			+10		MATCH	PAR /STAB.	PAR	METRES
10	237	4	18	6			4			18	18	4	225
11	510	5	14/26	6			5			4	7	5	482
12	281	4	16/32	4			4			10	9	4	256
13	355	4	2/21	6			4			2	2	4	322
14	147	3	10/31	5			3			16	16	3	110
15	532	5	6/19	7			6			8	11	5	391
16	395	4	4/23	4			3			6	4	4	360
17	190	3	8/28	3			5			12	13	3	148
18	281	4	17	6			4			14	15	4	239
IN	2928	36		47			38					36	2533
OUT	3080	36		49			42					37	2764
TOT	6008	72		96			80					73	5297
DEDUCT HANDICAP				30			17			ENTRY NO.			
NET TOTAL				66			63						

REPAIR BALL MARKS

STABLEFORD

Stableford is one of the most popular golf competitions. In a Stableford competition, you earn points depending on your score for each hole:

- An eagle (two under par) scores four points.
- A birdie (one under par) scores three points.
- A par scores two points.
- A bogey (one over par) scores one point.
- A double bogey (two over par) or worse scores no points.

If you are playing using handicaps, then before you begin the round each player must check his or her card to see on which hole(s) he or she receives strokes. You do this by using the Stroke/Stableford index column, or general index/rating column if there is no Stroke/Stableford column (see Figure 7). For example, a player with an 18 handicap receives one stroke on every hole, so if that player has a six on a par 5, he or she deducts one stroke, making it a net five, which is equivalent to par and earns the player two points. A player on a handicap of 25 receives one stroke on every hole and two strokes on holes 2, 5, 6, 8, 13, 15 and 16, rated 1 to 7 or 19 to 25 (see Figure 7). So if this player has five strokes on the fifteenth hole, this becomes a net three, which is an eagle and earns four points.

Each player should asterisk or circle the holes on which they receive one or two strokes. On your scorecard you should record your actual stroke score for each hole and next to this your point score, taking your handicap into consideration (see Figure 7). You should then total your points for each nine holes and for the full 18 holes. The winner is the player with the most points.

There are two major advantages to Stableford competition. The first is that even if you have one or two bad holes, this need not wreck your round because you can pick up a three- or four-point score on a good hole. The second is that Stableford is quick because once you have had more strokes than can earn a point on that hole, you simply pick up your ball and go to the next hole. You should only finish a hole if you can earn a point.

Par

A Par competition is similar to Stableford in that the player's handicap is applied to his/her Stroke score to earn wins, losses or halves for each hole. As with Stableford, before you begin your round you circle or asterisk the holes on which you receive strokes according to the Stroke Par index column (not par for each hole column), or general index/rating column if there is no Par index on the scorecard (see Figure 8). For example, a player with a 22 handicap receives one stroke on every hole except holes 5, 8, 13 and 15, where the player receives two strokes. If

Player(s) Paul McKernan

Home Club Kingston Dunes

MENS				PLAYER			MARKER			LADIES			
HOLE	METRES	PAR	RATING		+10			+10		MATCH	PAR/STAB.	PAR	METRES
1	195	3	3/30	5	1					17	12	3	150
2	350	4	5/(24)	6	2					9	1	4	306
3	344	4	12/29	4	3					13	12	4	272
4	154	3	13	4	2					7	6	3	135
5	392	4	1/(20)	6	2					15	17	5	386
6	495	5	15/(25)	7	2					5	8	5	442
7	362	4	7/27	4	3					3	3	4	345
8	476	5	11/(22)	7	2					1	5	5	428
9	312	4	9	6	1					11	10	4	300
OUT	3080	36			18							37	2764

Player PMcK

Marker D. Davis

Date 5/10/99

PLEASE REPAIR DIVOTS WITH SAND

Figure 7: Individual Stableford. The holes where the player receives two strokes are circled.

HANDICAP
25

COURSE	✓	A.C.R.	A.L.C.R.	C.C.R.	SCORE
MENS		71			35
LADIES			73		

MENS				PLAYER			MARKER			LADIES			
HOLE	METRES	PAR	RATING		+ – 0			+ – 0		MATCH	PAR /STAB.	PAR	METRES
10	237	4	18	4	3					18	18	4	225
11	510	5	14/26	5	3					4	7	5	482
12	281	4	16/32	5	2					10	9	4	256
13	355	4	2/21	5	3					2	2	4	322
14	147	3	10/31	5	1					16	16	3	110
15	532	5	6/19	8	1					8	11	5	391
16	395	4	4/23	5	3					6	4	4	360
17	190	3	8/28	6	–					12	13	3	148
18	281	4	17	6	1					14	15	4	239
IN	2928	36			17							36	2533
OUT	3080	36			18							37	2764
TOT	6008	72			35							73	5297
DEDUCT HANDICAP										ENTRY NO.			
NET TOTAL													

REPAIR BALL MARKS

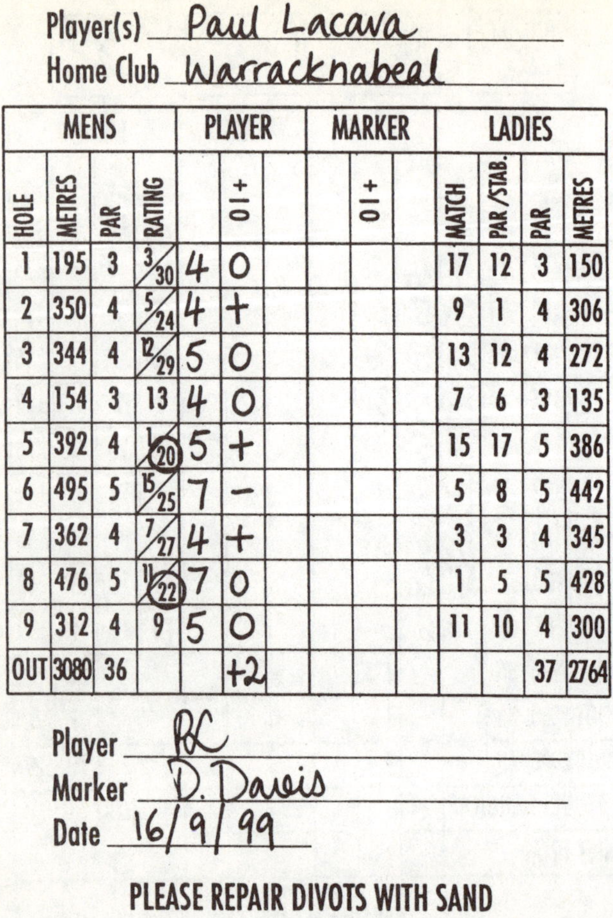
Player(s) Paul Lacava

Home Club Warracknabeal

MENS				PLAYER			MARKER			LADIES			
HOLE	METRES	PAR	RATING		+ 0 –			+ 0 –		MATCH	PAR /STAB.	PAR	METRES
1	195	3	3/30	4	0					17	12	3	150
2	350	4	5/24	4	+					9	1	4	306
3	344	4	12/29	5	0					13	12	4	272
4	154	3	13	4	0					7	6	3	135
5	392	4	1/(20)	5	+					15	17	5	386
6	495	5	15/25	7	–					5	8	5	442
7	362	4	7/27	4	+					3	3	4	345
8	476	5	11/(22)	7	0					1	5	5	428
9	312	4	9	5	0					11	10	4	300
OUT	3080	36			+2							37	2764

Player PC

Marker D. Davis

Date 16/9/99

PLEASE REPAIR DIVOTS WITH SAND

Figure 8: Individual Par scorecard. The holes where the player receives two strokes are circled.

HANDICAP
22

COURSE	✓	A.C.R.	A.L.C.R.	C.C.R.	SCORE
MENS		71			+4
LADIES			73		

MENS				PLAYER			MARKER			LADIES			
HOLE	METRES	PAR	RATING		+ − 0			+ − 0		MATCH	PAR /STAB.	PAR	METRES
10	237	4	18	4	+					18	18	4	225
11	510	5	14/26	7	−					4	7	5	482
12	281	4	16/32	5	0					10	9	4	256
13	355	4	2/21	6	0					2	2	4	322
14	147	3	10/31	3	+					16	16	3	110
15	532	5	6/19	8	−					8	11	5	391
16	395	4	4/23	4	+					6	4	4	360
17	190	3	8/28	4	0					12	13	3	148
18	281	4	17	4	+					14	15	4	239
IN	2928	36			+2							36	2533
OUT	3080	36			+2							37	2764
TOT	6008	72			+4							73	5297
DEDUCT HANDICAP										ENTRY NO.			
NET TOTAL													

REPAIR BALL MARKS

this player then had a five on the fifth hole, this would become a net four, which is a birdie. If he or she had five strokes on the 12th, this would become a net four, which is a par.

On the scorecard you record your actual number of strokes for each hole and next to it your result. If your net (handicap adjusted) score is a birdie or better, your result is a plus (+) or a win. If your net score is par, your result is a zero (0) and you have halved or squared the hole. If your net score is a bogey or worse your result is a minus (–) or a loss.

NET SCORE	RESULT	CARD
Birdie or better	Plus (win)	+
Par	Halved/squared	0
Bogey or worse	Minus (loss)	–

At the end of each nine holes and at the end of the round, you calculate your score by subtracting the number of minuses from the number of pluses. If you have more minuses than pluses, your result will be a negative figure. If you have more pluses than minuses, your result will be a positive figure (see Figure 8) and if you have the same number of pluses as minuses, your result will be zero. A plus result is called an 'up', a minus is a 'down' and a zero means the hole is halved. So +4 means you are four up or –2 means you are two down, whilst an overall result of zero means you were square.

The main disadvantage of Par competition is that

if you shoot a birdie and your net result is an eagle, you receive no extra benefit, just a plus. The main advantage of Par competition is that play is quick because you should not finish a hole if you cannot score a net par. On these holes you fill in your stroke score as a dash (—) and your result as a minus (–).

Bisque Par

Bisque Par competition is a variation on individual Par. In Bisque Par, instead of using the Stroke Par index to allocate your handicap strokes before your round, you do it on a hole by hole basis. In Bisque Par you can allot any number of your handicap strokes to any hole, as long as you make your decision before each hole and write it on your card. For example, your confidence might be down and on the 15th hole you have to play over and around a water hazard. Before you tee off, you allot three handicap strokes to this hole just in case you go into the 'drink'. So if the 15th hole is a Par 5 and you take eight strokes, you record a '0' (half). (See Figure 9.)

Of course, you have a limited number of handicap strokes to play with and once you use them all up, you play the remaining holes using your gross score for each. The winner is the player with the highest number of pluses — this is usually the player who is most consistent and the best at allotting strokes to holes that cause him or her trouble.

Player(s) Neil Buszard

Home Club Rosanna

MENS				PLAYER			MARKER			LADIES			
HOLE	METRES	PAR	RATING		+0–	Handicap strokes ↓		+0–		MATCH	PAR /STAB.	PAR	METRES
1	195	3	3/30	4	0	1				17	12	3	150
2	350	4	5/24	5	0	1				9	1	4	306
3	344	4	12/29	3	+	0				13	12	4	272
4	154	3	13	3	0	0				7	6	3	135
5	392	4	1/20	6	0	2				15	17	5	386
6	495	5	15/25	5	0	0				5	8	5	442
7	362	4	7/27	4	+	1				3	3	4	345
8	476	5	11/22	5	+	1				1	5	5	428
9	312	4	9	5	0	1				11	10	4	300
OUT	3080	36			+3	7						37	2764

Player NBuszard

Marker LDavis

Date 24/10/99

PLEASE REPAIR DIVOTS WITH SAND

Figure 9: Bisque Par scorecard

HANDICAP
13

COURSE	✓	A.C.R.	A.L.C.R.	C.C.R.	SCORE
MENS		71			+1
LADIES			73		

MENS				PLAYER			MARKER			LADIES			
HOLE	METRES	PAR	RATING		+0-	Handicap Strokes ↓		+0-		MATCH	PAR /STAB.	PAR	METRES
10	237	4	18	4	+	1				18	18	4	225
11	510	5	14/26	5	0	0				4	7	5	482
12	281	4	16/32	5	0	1				10	9	4	256
13	355	4	2/21	5	0	1				2	2	4	322
14	147	3	10/31	3	0	0				16	16	3	110
15	532	5	6/19	8	0	3				8	11	5	391
16	395	4	4/23	5	–	0				6	4	4	360
17	190	3	8/28	4	–	0				12	13	3	148
18	281	4	17	5	–	0				14	15	4	239
IN	2928	36			-2	6						36	2533
OUT	3080	36			+3							37	2764
TOT	6008	72			+1							73	5297
DEDUCT HANDICAP										ENTRY NO.			
NET TOTAL													

REPAIR BALL MARKS

Match Play

Match Play is a real player against player competition. In Match Play, the game is scored by holes rather than by strokes or points. You win a hole by holing your ball in the least number of strokes, which is recorded as a win or plus (+). If you both score the same, the hole is halved and the result is a zero (0) and if you lose a hole the result is a loss or minus (–). (See Figure 10.)

The score is expressed as the number of holes you are in front in relation to the number of holes still to be played. For example, four holes up and 11 holes to play is called four and 11. If the number of holes each player has won is even, the match is 'all square'. If one player gets so far in front that his or her opponent cannot catch up — for example six holes up with five holes to play — then the match is finished. The player has won the match 6/5.

If you play Match Play competition using your handicap, then on each hole the lower net (adjusted) score wins the hole. For example, if you take six strokes but get one stroke according to your handicap, your net score is five. If your opponent takes five but does not get a handicap stroke, he or she scores a net five. The result is that this hole is halved.

To calculate on which holes you receive strokes, first of all you must work out the difference between your handicap and your opponent's handicap. For example, if you have a ten handicap and your opponent's is 20, then you give your opponent ten strokes. You then use the Match Play or general rating index on the scorecard to work out which are the ten hardest holes on which your opponent receives a stroke. In Figure 10, Max Crow, who has a handicap of 13, gives Damien Davis, who has a handicap of 15, two strokes. One on hole five and one on hole 13.

One advantage of Match Play is that it is quick. You do not bother to finish a hole if you cannot halve it and if you work your way into an unbeatable position — for example four holes up three to play — the match is over and you do not bother to play the last three holes.

Match Play creates a lot of pressure because you need to counter all your opponent's moves. For example, if your opponent duffs his or her drive you need to hit a gem. If your opponent hits a superb second to within three metres, you really need to do likewise. In Match Play, pars and birdies lose any significance — you just need to have fewer strokes on each hole than your opponent. If your opponent takes a net nine, you only need a net eight to win the hole.

Player(s) Max Crow

Home Club The National

MENS				PLAYER			MARKER			LADIES			
HOLE	METRES	PAR	RATING		+ 0 −			+ 0 −		MATCH	PAR /STAB.	PAR	METRES
1	195	3	3/30	4	0		4	0		17	12	3	150
2	350	4	5/24	6	−		5	+		9	1	4	306
3	344	4	12/29	4	0		4	0		13	12	4	272
4	154	3	13	3	+		5	−		7	6	3	135
5	392	4	(1)/20	5	0		6	0		15	17	5	386
6	495	5	15/25	7	−		5	+		5	8	5	442
7	362	4	7/27	4	0		4	0		3	3	4	345
8	476	5	11/22	6	+		7	−		1	5	5	428
9	312	4	9	5	0		5	0		11	10	4	300
OUT	3080	36			0			0				37	2764

Player MCrow

Marker D. Davis (Handicap 15)

Date 3/8/99

PLEASE REPAIR DIVOTS WITH SAND

Figure 10: Individual Match Play. Holes where Damien Davis receives a stroke are circled.

HANDICAP
13

COURSE	✓	A.C.R.	A.L.C.R.	C.C.R.	SCORE
MENS		71			
LADIES			73		

MENS				PLAYER			MARKER			LADIES			
HOLE	METRES	PAR	RATING		+0−			+0−		MATCH	PAR /STAB.	PAR	METRES
10	237	4	18	4	0		4	0		18	18	4	225
11	510	5	14/26	6	−		5	+		4	7	5	482
12	281	4	16/32	5	−		4	+		10	9	4	256
13	355	4	(2)/21	5	−		5	+		2	2	4	322
14	147	3	10/31	3	0		3	0		16	16	3	110
15	532	5	6/19	7	0		7	0		8	11	5	391
16	395	4	4/23	4	0		4	0		6	4	4	360
17	190	3	8/28	Davis wins 3 up						12	13	3	148
18	281	4	17	with 2 holes						14	15	4	239
IN	2928	36		to play								36	2533
OUT	3080	36										37	2764
TOT	6008	72										73	5297
DEDUCT HANDICAP										ENTRY NO.			
NET TOTAL													

REPAIR BALL MARKS

Player(s) Gerry Davis (Lady member)

Home Club

MENS				PLAYER			MARKER			LADIES			
HOLE	METRES	PAR	RATING		+ − 0			+ − 0		MATCH	PAR /STAB.	PAR	METRES
1	195	3	3/30	5						17	12	3	150
2	350	4	5/24	8	13					9	1	4	306
3	344	4	12/29	7	20					13	12	4	272
4	154	3	13	5	25					7	6	3	135
5	392	4	1/20	5	30					15	17	5	386
6	495	5	15/25	7	37					5	8	5	442
7	362	4	7/27	6	43					3	3	4	345
8	476	5	11/22	6	49					1	5	5	428
9	312	4	9	6	55					11	10	4	300
OUT	3080	36		55								37	2764

Player GD

Marker D. Davis

Date 10/7/99

PLEASE REPAIR DIVOTS WITH SAND

Figure 11: Flag Competition scorecard

HANDICAP
33

COURSE	✓	A.C.R.	A.L.C.R.	C.C.R.	SCORE
MENS		71			Strokes 72+33=105
LADIES			73	Bunker 18th green	

MENS				PLAYER			MARKER			LADIES			
HOLE	METRES	PAR	RATING		+10			+10		MATCH	PAR /STAB.	PAR	METRES
10	237	4	18	5	60					18	18	4	225
11	510	5	14/26	7	67					4	7	5	482
12	281	4	16/32	5	72					10	9	4	256
13	355	4	2/21	8	80					2	2	4	322
14	147	3	10/31	5	85					16	16	3	110
15	532	5	6/19	7	92					8	11	5	391
16	395	4	4/23	5	97					6	4	4	360
17	190	3	8/28	3	100					12	13	3	148
18	281	4	17	5	105	Finished in greenside bunker				14	15	4	239
IN	2928	36		50								36	2533
OUT	3080	36		55								37	2764
TOT	6008	72		105								73	5297
DEDUCT HANDICAP										ENTRY NO.			
NET TOTAL													

REPAIR BALL MARKS

Flag Competition

A Flag Competition is a variation on Stroke Play and can be played as a large group tournament or in a group of four. Each player is allowed to have the number of strokes equal to par for the course plus his or her handicap. So if par for the course is 71 and your handicap is 24, you are allowed 95 strokes. The idea is to get as far around the course as possible in your allotted number of strokes.

The first player in a Flag Competition carries a flag and plants it on the spot where he or she completed their full number of strokes. The player then records his or her name on the flag. From then on, the players who follow who have not completed their strokes when they reach the flag take it with them until they run out of strokes. They plant the flag on the edge of the fairway, level with where their ball finished, and record their name on it. The player who carries the flag the longest distance from the first tee in his or her allotted number of strokes is the winner. The flag may finish somewhere short of the 18th green, or on the first or second hole of the second round.

You complete your scorecard by recording the number of strokes you take for each hole until you have used up your full stroke allotment (see Figure 11, previous page). As in all golf competitions, Flag relies on complete honesty in your scoring.

TEAM EVENTS

Four Ball Best Ball Stableford

The same scoring system is used for this event as in the individual Stableford event (see page 28). Players retain their individual handicaps throughout the round, however on each hole only one member of the pair records their score on the card (see Figure 12). This is always the player who scored the most points for that hole. For example, in Figure 12 Cameron McKenzie pars the first hole and so gets two points. However, on the 5th hole David Ackerly has five strokes, which is a net three strokes and three points for a birdie. In the case where both team members score the same points, the first person to putt out records their score.

Some interesting tactics can come into this event. For example, if your partner has already putted out for a net par (two points) and you have a putt for a net birdie (three points), you should putt aggressively because it doesn't matter if you miss, as your partner has already registered a net par.

Similarly, if you are having a shocking hole or your partner sinks a long putt and there is no way you can beat his or her net score, then you should pick up your ball and not bother to finish the hole.

Player(s) C. McKenzie (6) / D. Ackerly (22)

Home Club

MENS				PLAYER			MARKER			LADIES			
HOLE	METRES	PAR	RATING	C.Mc	0 | +	D.A.		0 | +		MATCH	PAR /STAB.	PAR	METRES
1	195	3	3/30	4/2	2					17	12	3	150
2	350	4	5/24	5/2	2					9	1	4	306
3	344	4	12/29		3	4/3				13	12	4	272
4	154	3	13		2	4/2				7	6	3	135
5	392	4	1/(20)		3	5/3				15	17	5	386
6	495	5	15/25	5/2	2					5	8	5	442
7	362	4	7/27	3/3	3					3	3	4	345
8	476	5	11/(22)		2	7/2				1	5	5	428
9	312	4	9	3/3	3					11	10	4	300
OUT	3080	36			22							37	2764

Player C McKenzie D Ackerly

Marker S Blackman

Date 4/3/99

PLEASE REPAIR DIVOTS WITH SAND

Figure 12: Four Ball Best Ball Stableford. Holes where David Ackerly gets two strokes are circled.

HANDICAP
6/22

COURSE	✓	A.C.R.	A.L.C.R.	C.C.R.	SCORE
MENS		71			42 points
LADIES			73		

MENS				PLAYER			MARKER			LADIES			
HOLE	METRES	PAR	RATING	C.Mc	+ – 0	D.A.		+ – 0		MATCH	PAR /STAB.	PAR	METRES
10	237	4	18	4/2	2					18	18	4	225
11	510	5	14/26		3	5/3				4	7	5	482
12	281	4	16/32		2	5/2				10	9	4	256
13	355	4	2/(21)		4	4/4				2	2	4	322
14	147	3	10/31		1	5/1				16	16	3	110
15	532	5	6/(19)	6/2	2					8	11	5	391
16	395	4	4/23	4/3	3					6	4	4	360
17	190	3	8/28	4/1	1					12	13	3	148
18	281	4	17	4/2	2					14	15	4	239
IN	2928	36			20							36	2533
OUT	3080	36			22							37	2764
TOT	6008	72			42	pts						73	5297
DEDUCT HANDICAP										ENTRY NO.			
NET TOTAL													

REPAIR BALL MARKS

This speeds up the game, as there is no point continuing to play the hole if your partner will definitely better your net score.

Pairs Aggregate Stableford

This event is played with a partner, using the Stableford scoring system. Individual handicaps are used throughout the round and both partners' Stableford scores are added together at the end of each hole to find the total points achieved by the team (pair) for that hole. For example, in Figure 13, on the first hole both Paul and Graham Blackman score bogies which, with handicap adjustment, become net pars (two points each) giving them a total of four points. At the end of the round, the total combined points are calculated and recorded at the top of the card, as in Figure 13.

This event puts pressure on all players, as you do not want to let your partner down since both of your scores count. In this competition you only pick up your ball if you cannot score a point on the hole.

Four Ball Best Ball Par

This event uses the same scoring system as the individual Par competition (see page 29). Individual handicaps are used for the duration of the event, however only the best score in your pair for each hole is recorded on the card. If partners have the same score, only the partner who holed out first is recorded on the card. On the scorecard (see Figure 14) you record the stroke score for the best ball on each hole and the result: plus (+) or minus (–) or zero (0).

This is a time-saving game, for you should pick up your ball if you are not able to make a net par or your partner has holed out for a score better than you can obtain for that hole.

This event allows you to work as a team, because if one player is sure of getting a half (net par), the other player can be more aggressive and attempt a plus (net birdie or better).

Player(s) P. Blackman (6) / G. Blackman (12)

Home Club Riversdale

MENS				PLAYER			MARKER			LADIES			
HOLE	METRES	PAR	RATING	P.B.	+ 0 −	G.B.		+ 0 −		MATCH	PAR /STAB.	PAR	METRES
1	195	3	3/30	4/2	4	4/2				17	12	3	150
2	350	4	5/24	–	3	4/3				9	1	4	306
3	344	4	12/29	4/2	5	4/3				13	12	4	272
4	154	3	13	3/2	4	3/2				7	6	3	135
5	392	4	1/20	4/3	4	6/1				15	17	5	386
6	495	5	15/25	6/1	2	6/1				5	8	5	442
7	362	4	7/27	4/2	2	–				3	3	4	345
8	476	5	11/22	5/2	5	5/3				1	5	5	428
9	312	4	9	4/2	5	4/3				11	10	4	300
OUT	3080	36		16	(34)	18						37	2764

Player P Blackman

Marker D. Davis

Date 10/1/99

PLEASE REPAIR DIVOTS WITH SAND

Figure 13: **Pairs Aggregate Stableford scorecard**

HANDICAP
6/12

COURSE	✓	A.C.R.	A.L.C.R.	C.C.R.	SCORE
MENS		71			71 points
LADIES			73		

MENS				PLAYER			MARKER			LADIES			
HOLE	METRES	PAR	RATING	P.B.	+ 0 −	G.B.		+ 0 −		MATCH	PAR /STAB.	PAR	METRES
10	237	4	18	3/3	4	5/1				18	18	4	225
11	510	5	14/26	4/3	5	5/2				4	7	5	482
12	281	4	16/32	4/2	3	5/1				10	9	4	256
13	355	4	2/21	4/3	5	5/2				2	2	4	322
14	147	3	10/31	4/1	3	4/2				16	16	3	110
15	532	5	6/19	5/3	6	5/3				8	11	5	391
16	395	4	4/23	4/3	6	4/3				6	4	4	360
17	190	3	8/28	4/1	1	–				12	13	3	148
18	281	4	17	4/2	4	4/2				14	15	4	239
IN	2928	36		21	(37)	16						36	2533
OUT	3080	36		16	34	18						37	2764
TOT	6008	72		37	(71)	34						73	5297
DEDUCT HANDICAP										ENTRY NO.			
NET TOTAL													

REPAIR BALL MARKS

Player(s) D. Bayliss (20) / R. Berryman (21)

Home Club Spring Valley

MENS				PLAYER			MARKER			LADIES			
HOLE	METRES	PAR	RATING	DB	+/−/0	RB		+/−/0		MATCH	PAR /STAB.	PAR	METRES
1	195	3	3/30	4	0					17	12	3	150
2	350	4	5/24	5	0					9	1	4	306
3	344	4	12/29		+	4				13	12	4	272
4	154	3	13		0	4				7	6	3	135
5	392	4	1/(20)	5	+					15	17	5	386
6	495	5	15/25	–	–	–				5	8	5	442
7	362	4	7/27		+	4				3	3	4	345
8	476	5	11/22		+	5				1	5	5	428
9	312	4	9	5	0					11	10	4	300
OUT	3080	36			+3							37	2764

Player D Bayliss

Marker S Blackman

Date 15/9/99

PLEASE REPAIR DIVOTS WITH SAND

Figure 14: Four Ball Best Ball Par scorecard. Holes where Berryman gets two strokes are circled.

HANDICAP
20/21

COURSE	✓	A.C.R.	A.L.C.R.	C.C.R.	SCORE
MENS		71			+6
LADIES			73		

MENS				PLAYER			MARKER			LADIES			
HOLE	METRES	PAR	RATING	DB	+0−	RB		+0−		MATCH	PAR /STAB.	PAR	METRES
10	237	4	18		0	5				18	18	4	225
11	510	5	14/26	6	0					4	7	5	482
12	281	4	16/32	4	+					10	9	4	256
13	355	4	2/21		0	6				2	2	4	322
14	147	3	10/31		0	4				16	16	3	110
15	532	5	6/19	7	0					8	11	5	391
16	395	4	4/23		+	4				6	4	4	360
17	190	3	8/28		+	3				12	13	3	148
18	281	4	17		0	5				14	15	4	239
IN	2928	36			+3							36	2533
OUT	3080	36			+3							37	2764
TOT	6008	72			+6							73	5297
DEDUCT HANDICAP										ENTRY NO.			
NET TOTAL													

REPAIR BALL MARKS

Four Ball Best Ball Stroke

This competition is basically scored in the same way as an individual Stroke competition, with each player using his or her individual handicap. The difference is that you are playing with a partner, and only the best net score for that hole is recorded on the scorecard.

On the scorecard you record the gross score and the net score for the partner with the best score on each hole. For example, in Figure 15 Mark Hibbins had a gross four on the first hole, which according to his handicap is a net three. On the second hole, Scott Blackman had a gross three, which is a net two according to his handicap. If both players have the same net score for that hole, then the player who holed out first has their score recorded on the card. At the end of the round, you total up the best net stroke score for each hole and this is filled in as your result at the top of the card (see Figure 15).

A crucial difference between this and Individual Stroke is that you are allowed to pick up your ball if there is no way you can better your partner's score. This assists in making a Four Ball Best Ball Stroke round much quicker than an individual Stroke round.

FOURSOMES

This is a stroke event played with pairs, where partners play one ball and alternate shots. For example, player one hits the tee shot, then player two the second shot, and so on until the ball is holed out. Tee shots must be alternated throughout the round (ie, one player tees off on all the even holes whilst the other player tees off on all the odd holes).

A team's handicap is found by adding both players' handicaps together then dividing by two. For example, in Figure 16 partners have handicaps of 8 and 20, giving a combined handicap of 28 ÷ 2 = 14. The stroke score for each hole is filled in on the card and at the end of 18 holes, the gross and net totals are calculated. The pair with the lowest net score wins the competition.

Foursomes is a great game to play if you know your partner well, but can become frustrating if your partner is not having a good day or you feel you are making it difficult for your partner by playing poor shots. It is a good game to play on a course you play all the time, as your partner is likely to put you in positions you have never been in before.

Foursomes is also a very quick game if played properly, as one player can be walking to where the next shot is (supposed to be) heading. The only problem with this competition is that players only play half the number of shots they would play in a normal round.

Player(s) S. Blackman (9) / M. Hibbins (15)

Home Club Flinders

MENS				PLAYER			MARKER			LADIES			
HOLE	METRES	PAR	RATING	SB	~~NETT~~	MH		0–+		MATCH	PAR/STAB.	PAR	METRES
1	195	3	3/30		3	4				17	12	3	150
2	350	4	5/24	3	2					9	1	4	306
3	344	4	12/29		4	5				13	12	4	272
4	154	3	13	4	4					7	6	3	135
5	392	4	1/20	6	5					15	17	5	386
6	495	5	15/25		5	6				5	8	5	442
7	362	4	7/27	5	4					3	3	4	345
8	476	5	11/22		5	6				1	5	5	428
9	312	4	9		3	4				11	10	4	300
OUT	3080	36			35							37	2764

Player SBlackman

Marker D. Davis

Date 5/6/99

PLEASE REPAIR DIVOTS WITH SAND

Figure 15: Four Ball Best Ball Stroke scorecard

HANDICAP
9/15

COURSE	✓	A.C.R.	A.L.C.R.	C.C.R.	SCORE
MENS		71			67
LADIES			73		

MENS				PLAYER			MARKER			LADIES			
HOLE	METRES	PAR	RATING	SB	NEAT	MH		+ − 0		MATCH	PAR /STAB.	PAR	METRES
10	237	4	18		4	4				18	18	4	225
11	510	5	14/26		4	5				4	7	5	482
12	281	4	16/32	4	4					10	9	4	256
13	355	4	2/21	5	4					2	2	4	322
14	147	3	10/31	3	3					16	16	3	110
15	532	5	6/19		4	5				8	11	5	391
16	395	4	4/23	4	3					6	4	4	360
17	190	3	8/28		2	3				12	13	3	148
18	281	4	17		4	4				14	15	4	239
IN	2928	36			32							36	2533
OUT	3080	36			35							37	2764
TOT	6008	72			67							73	5297
DEDUCT HANDICAP										ENTRY NO.			
NET TOTAL													

REPAIR BALL MARKS

Player(s) B. Harper (8) / R. Ashman (20)

Home Club Lakeside

MENS				PLAYER			MARKER			LADIES			
HOLE	METRES	PAR	RATING		0 – +			0 – +		MATCH	PAR /STAB.	PAR	METRES
1	195	3	3/30	4						17	12	3	150
2	350	4	5/24	6						9	1	4	306
3	344	4	12/29	4						13	12	4	272
4	154	3	13	3						7	6	3	135
5	392	4	1/20	5						15	17	5	386
6	495	5	15/25	5						5	8	5	442
7	362	4	7/27	5						3	3	4	345
8	476	5	11/22	6						1	5	5	428
9	312	4	9	4						11	10	4	300
OUT	3080	36		42								37	2764

Player B. Harper

Marker D. Davis

Date 15/10/99

PLEASE REPAIR DIVOTS WITH SAND

Figure 16: **Foursomes scorecard**

HANDICAP
8/20 (14)

COURSE	✓	A.C.R.	A.L.C.R.	C.C.R.	SCORE
MENS		71			72
LADIES			73		

MENS				PLAYER			MARKER			LADIES			
HOLE	METRES	PAR	RATING		+/-			+/-		MATCH	PAR /STAB.	PAR	METRES
10	237	4	18	4						18	18	4	225
11	510	5	14/26	5						4	7	5	482
12	281	4	16/32	5						10	9	4	256
13	355	4	2/21	6						2	2	4	322
14	147	3	10/31	3						16	16	3	110
15	532	5	6/19	5						8	11	5	391
16	395	4	4/23	6						6	4	4	360
17	190	3	8/28	4						12	13	3	148
18	281	4	17	6						14	15	4	239
IN	2928	36		44								36	2533
OUT	3080	36		42								37	2764
TOT	6008	72		86								73	5297
DEDUCT HANDICAP				14						ENTRY NO.			
NET TOTAL				72									

REPAIR BALL MARKS

Canadian Foursomes

This is a pairs event and is played using the stroke scoring method. Both players tee-off, then the ball in the best position is chosen and the other ball is picked up. The player who did not hit the ball that was chosen must hit the second shot, and alternate shots are played from there until the ball is holed.

The team handicap is found by adding both players' individual handicaps together and then dividing by two. For example, in Figure 17 partners have handicaps of 16 and 12 so their Canadian Foursomes handicap is 28 ÷ 2 = 14. The stroke score for each hole is recorded on the card, and after 18 holes the gross and net totals are calculated.

This event is an excellent variation on the Foursomes game as it allows both players to tee off every hole, thus having more shots during the round.

American Foursomes

Being a Foursome event, this competition is played with a partner, using the stroke scoring method. Here, both players tee-off and then proceed to play each other's ball for their second shot. After the second shot, the pair decide which ball is in the best position and the other ball is picked up. Play then proceeds as in normal Foursomes, where if the second shot of player two is the chosen ball, player one will now hit the third.

Handicaps for male teams are determined by adding the players' individual handicaps and dividing by two. For mixed and ladies play, add the players' handicaps and multiply by ⅜. The stroke score for each hole is recorded on the card (see Figure 18) and after 18 holes the gross and net totals are calculated.

This is a very interesting variation on Foursomes, but it can become difficult to decide which ball is in the best position. For example, a ball 160 metres from the green is in a better position than a ball five metres from the green right behind a tree, but you often don't know that until you reach your ball. This can lead to some very long rounds.

Player(s) S. Avery (16) / G. Blackman (12)

Home Club

MENS				PLAYER			MARKER			LADIES			
HOLE	METRES	PAR	RATING		+ – 0			+ – 0		MATCH	PAR /STAB.	PAR	METRES
1	195	3	3/30	4						17	12	3	150
2	350	4	5/24	5						9	1	4	306
3	344	4	12/29	4						13	12	4	272
4	154	3	13	3						7	6	3	135
5	392	4	1/20	6						15	17	5	386
6	495	5	15/25	7						5	8	5	442
7	362	4	7/27	3						3	3	4	345
8	476	5	11/22	5						1	5	5	428
9	312	4	9	4						11	10	4	300
OUT	3080	36		41								37	2764

Player S.A.

Marker D. Davis

Date 30/10/99

PLEASE REPAIR DIVOTS WITH SAND

Figure 17: Canadian Foursomes scorecard

HANDICAP	COURSE	✓	A.C.R.	A.L.C.R.	C.C.R.	SCORE
16/12 (14)	MENS		71			69
	LADIES			73		

MENS				PLAYER			MARKER			LADIES			
HOLE	METRES	PAR	RATING		+10			+10		MATCH	PAR/STAB.	PAR	METRES
10	237	4	18	4						18	18	4	225
11	510	5	14/26	6						4	7	5	482
12	281	4	16/32	5						10	9	4	256
13	355	4	2/21	5						2	2	4	322
14	147	3	10/31	4						16	16	3	110
15	532	5	6/19	6						8	11	5	391
16	395	4	4/23	4						6	4	4	360
17	190	3	8/28	4						12	13	3	148
18	281	4	17	4						14	15	4	239
IN	2928	36		42								36	2533
OUT	3080	36		41								37	2764
TOT	6008	72		83								73	5297
DEDUCT HANDICAP				14						ENTRY NO.			
NET TOTAL				69									

REPAIR BALL MARKS

Player(s) D.Baker (22) / G. Irvine (18)

Home Club —

MENS				PLAYER			MARKER			LADIES			
HOLE	METRES	PAR	RATING		0 − +			0 − +		MATCH	PAR/STAB.	PAR	METRES
1	195	3	3/30	4						17	12	3	150
2	350	4	5/24	5						9	1	4	306
3	344	4	12/29	5						13	12	4	272
4	154	3	13	5						7	6	3	135
5	392	4	1/20	6						15	17	5	386
6	495	5	15/25	6						5	8	5	442
7	362	4	7/27	5						3	3	4	345
8	476	5	11/22	6						1	5	5	428
9	312	4	9	6						11	10	4	300
OUT	3080	36		48								37	2764

Player D Baker

Marker [illegible]

Date 6/6/99

PLEASE REPAIR DIVOTS WITH SAND

Figure 18: American Foursomes scorecard

HANDICAP
22/18
(20)

COURSE	✓	A.C.R.	A.L.C.R.	C.C.R.	SCORE
MENS		71			72
LADIES			73		

MENS				PLAYER			MARKER			LADIES			
HOLE	METRES	PAR	RATING		+ – 0			+ – 0		MATCH	PAR /STAB.	PAR	METRES
10	237	4	18	4						18	18	4	225
11	510	5	14/26	6						4	7	5	482
12	281	4	16/32	5						10	9	4	256
13	355	4	2/21	5						2	2	4	322
14	147	3	10/31	4						16	16	3	110
15	532	5	6/19	6						8	11	5	391
16	395	4	4/23	5						6	4	4	360
17	190	3	8/28	3						12	13	3	148
18	281	4	17	6						14	15	4	239
IN	2928	36		44								36	2533
OUT	3080	36		48								37	2764
TOT	6008	72		92								73	5297
DEDUCT HANDICAP				20						ENTRY NO.			
NET TOTAL				72									

REPAIR BALL MARKS

AMBROSE (TWO, THREE AND FOUR BALL)

This event can be played in teams of two, three or four. Each member of the team hits off in order as determined by the team captain (the captain is usually the lowest handicapper). This order remains the same throughout the round. Once it has been decided which ball is in the best position, all other team members pick up their balls and drop them within one club length of the selected ball, no nearer to the hole. All team members hit from this position and once again decide which ball is in the best position to play the next stroke. This process continues until the ball is holed.

Some important rules:

- All team members must play from the same cut of grass or hazard in which the selected ball lies. For example, if the selected ball lies in the edge of a bunker, all players must play from the bunker, even though the fairway may be less than one club length from where the ball lies.
- On the putting surface, all team members must play from within 15 centimetres of the selected ball.
- No player may play their next shot until all players have attempted the previous shot. This most often occurs on the putting green when a putt finishes close to the hole and the player taps the putt in before other team members

have putted. This does not count and one of the other balls must be selected for the next shot.

The stroke score for each hole is marked on the card and after 18 holes the gross score is totalled.

Handicaps for Ambrose competition are as follows:

- Two Ball: both players' stroke handicaps are added, then divided by four.
- Three Ball: all players' stroke handicaps are added, then divided by six.
- Four Ball: all players' stroke handicaps are added, then divided by eight.

The handicap is subtracted from the gross score (see Figure 19) to give the net result.

All team members must have their name and handicap recorded on the card and the card must be signed by two members of the team.

Ambrose is an excellent competition to play when there are large numbers of players in a group (for example, sports teams on trips, etc). It provides for a fairly quick round and allows hackers to be a part of a score (usually) somewhere near par.

Player(s) S. Blackman (7) / S. Avery (14) /
Home Club T. Symons (10) / P. Blackman (9)

MENS				PLAYER			MARKER			LADIES			
HOLE	METRES	PAR	RATING		+10			+10		MATCH	PAR /STAB.	PAR	METRES
1	195	3	3/30	4						17	12	3	150
2	350	4	5/24	4						9	1	4	306
3	344	4	12/29	4						13	12	4	272
4	154	3	13	3						7	6	3	135
5	392	4	1/20	4						15	17	5	386
6	495	5	15/25	4						5	8	5	442
7	362	4	7/27	3						3	3	4	345
8	476	5	11/22	4						1	5	5	428
9	312	4	9	4						11	10	4	300
OUT	3080	36		34								37	2764

Player S Blackman P Blackman
Marker D. Davis
Date 4/10/99

PLEASE REPAIR DIVOTS WITH SAND

Figure 19: **Four Ball Ambrose scorecard**

HANDICAP
40/8 = 5

COURSE	✓	A.C.R.	A.L.C.R.	C.C.R.	SCORE
MENS		71			65
LADIES			73		

MENS				PLAYER			MARKER			LADIES			
HOLE	METRES	PAR	RATING		+ 0 −			+ 0 −		MATCH	PAR /STAB.	PAR	METRES
10	237	4	18	3						18	18	4	225
11	510	5	14/26	5						4	7	5	482
12	281	4	16/32	4						10	9	4	256
13	355	4	2/21	4						2	2	4	322
14	147	3	10/31	3						16	16	3	110
15	532	5	6/19	6						8	11	5	391
16	395	4	4/23	4						6	4	4	360
17	190	3	8/28	3						12	13	3	148
18	281	4	17	4						14	15	4	239
IN	2928	36		36								36	2533
OUT	3080	36		34								37	2764
TOT	6008	72		70								73	5297
DEDUCT HANDICAP				5						ENTRY NO.			
NET TOTAL				65									

REPAIR BALL MARKS

Four Ball Match Play

This event is very similar to individual Match Play (see page 38), except that here the competition involves two teams of two players.

Handicaps are worked out in the same way as individual Match Play, whereby the lowest handicap player is said to be playing off scratch (zero handicap), and the other players' handicaps are the difference between their handicap and the lowest handicap.

For example:

	Normal handicap	Four Ball Match Play Handicap
Player one	7	0
Player two	16	9
Player three	20	13
Player four	32	25

Strokes are taken as directed by the Match Play index or general index on the card, so in this case, player two would receive a stroke from player 1 on the holes rated 1–9 on the general rating index or Match Play index (see Figure 20, general rating index for men and Match Play index for women). At the end of each hole, the best net score for each pair determines their result. If the best net score is the same, then the hole is halved. If pair A has a lower net score, their result is a plus (+) win and pair B's is a minus (–) loss. The pair with the most pluses wins.

This event puts a lot of pressure on the low handicap players, because in many cases they are giving shots on every hole. It is a very good way of evening out four players.

Player(s) J. McKernan (18) / G. Davis (36)
Home Club B. Blackman (18) / H. Higginbotham (36)

MENS				PLAYER			MARKER			* LADIES			
HOLE	METRES	PAR	RATING	JMc	+ − 0	GD	HH	+ − 0	BB	MATCH	PAR /STAB.	PAR	METRES
1	195	3	3/30	4	0			0	4	17	12	3	150
2	350	4	5/24		+	6		−	6	9	1	4	306
3	344	4	12/29		0	6	6	0		13	12	4	272
4	154	3	13		+	3	4	−		7	6	3	135
5	392	4	1/20	6	−		6	+		15	17	5	386
6	495	5	15/25		+	6		−	6	5	8	5	442
7	362	4	7/27	6	−		6	+		3	3	4	345
8	476	5	11/22		0	6	6	0		1	5	5	428
9	312	4	9	5	0			0	5	11	10	4	300
OUT	3080	36			+1			−1				37	2764

Player J.Mc G. Davis
Marker BB HH
Date 1/11/99

PLEASE REPAIR DIVOTS WITH SAND

Figure 20: Four Ball Match Play scorecard

HANDICAP
18 / 36
18 / 36

COURSE	✓	A.C.R.	A.L.C.R.	C.C.R.	SCORE
MENS		71			JMcGD
LADIES			73		+1

MENS				PLAYER			MARKER			* LADIES			
HOLE	METRES	PAR	RATING	JMc	– 0 +	GD	HH	– 0 +	BB	MATCH	PAR /STAB.	PAR	METRES
10	237	4	18	5	0			0	5	18	18	4	225
11	510	5	14/26	6	–		6	+		4	7	5	482
12	281	4	16/32		+	6		–	6	10	9	4	256
13	355	4	2/21		+	6		–	6	2	2	4	322
14	147	3	10/31	4	0			0	4	16	16	3	110
15	532	5	6/19		0	7	7	0		8	11	5	391
16	395	4	4/23		0	6	6	0		6	4	4	360
17	190	3	8/28	4	–		4	+		12	13	3	148
18	281	4	17	6	0			0	6	14	15	4	239
IN	2928	36			0			0				36	2533
OUT	3080	36			+1			–1				37	2764
TOT	6008	72			+1			–1				73	5297
DEDUCT HANDICAP										ENTRY NO.			
NET TOTAL													

REPAIR BALL MARKS

GAMBLING GAMES

Most golfers are amateurs and so must adhere to the Rules of Amateur Status as published in the Royal and Ancient Golf Club of St Andrews (R&A) Rules of Golf. Basically, an amateur golfer is someone who plays the game as a non-profit making sport. However, the rules further state that wagering among individual golfers or teams is acceptable provided:

- The players involved advance all money won.
- The primary purpose is to play for enjoyment, not prize money.

There is a further regulation that cash prizes for amateur tournaments are unacceptable and the total value of prizes offered in an amateur tournament must not exceed $425 retail value. Rules books, which include The Rules of Amateur Status, are available from the Australian Golf Union (AGU), State Golf Associations and golf clubs. So the bottom line is that a bet here and there is fine, as long as things don't get out of hand. In fact, gambling has always been popular in golf and the following games give a myriad of ways to have a wager amongst your friends.

The Nassau

The golf ball Nassau is probably the most basic form of wager in golf. In four ball (four player) competitions, each player agrees to pay his or her opponents a golf ball each on the result of the first nine holes, a golf ball each on the result of the second nine holes and a golf ball each on the result of the full eighteen holes. This could cost you six balls, so sometimes the Nassau is changed to one ball per player on the first nine, second nine and eighteen. You may also wish to use money rather than balls as the wager and dollar, dollar, dollar is a popular version, which only costs you $6 if you lose both nines and the full 18 holes.

However, as with all gambling games, all players must agree on the wager before anyone tees off on the first hole, and you must make sure all players understand what they are up for if they lose. This will save an unpleasant argument later.

Drinks

Golf being such a time-consuming game and most popular in summer, you most probably follow a round with a few drinks at the bar or kiosk. In a Drinks game, you and your playing partners agree on a suitable wager, for example $5 each for each nine holes and the round. On completion of your match, the losers each put their $15 on the table to provide drinks for both themselves and the winners. If players do not drink all the money on the table, the left-over money is divided up by the winners.

DOUBLING

Doubling is not a game in itself, it is a method of recouping your losses in Nassau or Drinks. For example, you may decide to play a Nassau of one golf ball each for the first nine, second nine and total 18, with doubling allowed. At the end of the first nine, the losing pair can opt to double on the second nine. This means the second nine is played for two balls each, so if they win the second nine, they end up winning two balls each, which more than offsets the ball they lost on the first nine. However, if they lose the second nine as well, the damage is now greater.

Remember, the Doubling option must be agreed upon before you begin your round and it is an option only for the individual or pair who is losing the match.

SKINS

Skins has become a very popular gambling golf game in recent years due to the media coverage of professional Skins tournaments. However, apart from the standard of play, the big difference between these tournaments and your Skins match is that you are risking your own money and not playing to win the sponsor's money as the professionals do.

In a Skins match, you and your playing partners agree on an amount of money that each of you will put up on each hole, for example, 50 cents per hole would mean that if you didn't win a skin (hole) you would lose 18 x 50 cents = $9. If you are playing in a foursome, each skin (hole) will be worth $2.

To win a 'Skin' you have to win a hole outright. For example, if you take three strokes and the other players all take four strokes, you win that Skin (hole). Or if you all take five strokes, but you get a stroke on that hole due to your handicap, giving you a net four, you win the hole. If two or more players share the lowest score on a hole, no-one wins and the Skin jackpots to the next hole. So, for example, if no-one won the first five holes, the sixth hole would be worth six Skins, or $12. Or if you win the first two Skins, no-one wins the next four, the seventh hole will be worth five Skins or $10.

It's easiest to award the money at the end of the round. Each player puts in his or her $9 and Skins are awarded hole by hole to the winners.

Split Sixes

Split Sixes can only be played in a group of three. Before teeing-off players must agree on a suitable wager. There are a number of different types of wager possible with Split Sixes. For example:

- Losers pay the winner 20 cents per point.
- Each player puts in $5 and the highest point scorer takes all.
- Each player puts in $5 for each nine and $5 for the round, so the highest point-scorer on each nine and the full round wins $10.

Six points are awarded on each hole, but how the points are divided depends on the players' scores.

- If all players score the same, each player is awarded two points.
- If one player wins the hole outright, he or she is awarded four points. If the other two players have the same score, both of them receive one point each.
- If there is an outright winner, an outright second and a clear last on a hole, then the winner receives four points, the second receives two points, and the loser receives no points.
- If two players share the lowest score on a hole, then both of them receive three points each and the loser receives no points.

Points are totalled at the end of each nine and the end of the round, and all bets are then settled.

A variation to this scoring method is the addition of a proviso that if a player wins a hole outright by two or more strokes, that player wins the full six points for that hole.

The Snake

The Snake is an award received by you or one of your playing partners. There are two Snake types of award and you can choose to include one or both in your round of golf.

The first Snake is an award everyone tries to avoid. The first player in a round to three-putt on a hole wins the Snake. This player holds the Snake until someone else in the group three-putts on a hole. The player who has the Snake award at the end of the last hole must either shout drinks for all players, or pay each player a sum of money that was agreed upon before the round began. For example, you and your playing partners have decided on a $5 penalty to be paid to each player by the holder of the Snake. One player holds the Snake until the 16th hole, when both you and another player in your foursome three-putt. Now you hold the Snake because your three-putt was the last in the hole. No-one else three-putts on the last two holes, so you owe each player $5.

The second Snake award is more sought after. This is awarded to the player who makes the longest putt during the round. The first player to make a reasonable length putt holds the Snake until someone else drops a longer putt. At the end of the round, the holder of the longest putt Snake wins from each player a sum that was agreed upon before the round began.

Presents

In a Presents gambling game you win money from your playing partners for good shots. Presents is played in conjunction with normal Stroke, Stableford or Par and the amount of each Present, for example 20 cents from each player, is fixed before you tee off on the first hole. Presents can be won for all or any of the following, and you need to decide before you tee-off which Presents can be earned on that day:

- Nearest the pin on Par 3 holes.
- Longest drive on designated Par 4 or Par 5 holes.
- A one-putt on any green.
- Chip in from off the green.
- Out of the bunker in one shot followed by one putt into the hole. This is called a Sandy or a Camel.
- First player onto the green.
- Lowest score on the hardest hole in each nine holes.
- Lowest score on the easiest hole in each nine holes.

You need to keep a separate scorecard that records the Presents each player wins on each hole. At the end of the round, each player settles his or her debts by paying Presents to those who have earned them.

Bingle, Bongle, Bangle

This unusually named gambling game centres around the cut throat end of golf, 'the green'. In this game you win points every time you earn a Bingle, a Bongle or a Bangle.

A **Bingle** is earned if you are the first player in your group to get your ball onto the green, irrespective of score. For example, you may duff your first three shots so that you still have not reached the other players' drives, however your fourth shot is a gem and goes straight onto the green, so you win a Bingle. Notice that normal etiquette of furthest from the hole plays first must be adhered to in this game.

A **Bongle** is earned if all players are on the green and you are the nearest to the hole.

A **Bangle** is earned if you are the first player to put your ball in the hole, but remember that furthest from the hole must play first.

For the first six holes, each Bingle, Bongle or Bangle is worth one point. On holes seven to 12 each Bingle, Bongle or Bangle is worth two points, whilst on the holes 13–18, each is worth three points. Money changes hands at the end of the round, according to the payment method you and your partners agree upon before the round begins. The possibilities are:

- The highest point-scorer is paid a fixed amount by each player at the end of the round; or
- The total number of points earned by all players at the end of the round will be 108. This number is then divided by four and each player then puts this number of dollars ($27) into a pool. At the end of the round each player in turn draws from the pool the number of dollars equivalent to the number of points he or she won. For example, four players put in $27 each to make a total of $108. If the players scored 42, 38, 20 and eight points, the first player takes $42, the second $38, the third $20 and the fourth $8.

Pair Sums

This game is played in pairs and relies heavily on both partners scoring well. To score in Pair Sums, you combine both partners' stroke scores to form a two-digit number, putting the higher stroke score first, followed by the lower. For example, if you take a seven and your partner takes a five, your Pair Sum score is 75 for that hole.

Meanwhile, your opponents had a seven and a four, so their number on the same hole is 74. The lowest score wins the hole, so on this hole your opponents win. If you are using handicaps, then net stroke scores are used. For example, on the next hole you take an eight but you get a one-stroke deduction, so you have a net seven. Your partner has a seven but does not get any deductions on this hole, so your number is 77. Your opponents, however, both score eights but one opponent gets a two-stroke deduction, whilst the other receives a one-stroke deduction. Their scores therefore become 8 – 1 = 7 and 8 – 2 = 6, giving a number of 76, so you lose this hole.

In a Pair Sums match you bet on each hole. For example, you may decide before you tee off that each hole will be worth 50 cents each. At the end of the round, if one pair has won eight holes and their opponents ten holes, then the winners receive 2 x 50 cents from each opponent.

THE DUD

The Dud award is given to the player who makes the most glaring mistakes in a round. This is not an award anyone wants to win and it results in the recipient having to pay a penalty to other players. The penalty is decided upon before the round begins but is usually two rounds of drinks or a fee such as $2 to each player.

The receiver of the Dud award is the player who accumulates the highest number of points according to the following scoring system:

Fresh-air swing	5 pts
Lost ball	3 pts
Out of bounds	3 pts
In the water	2 pts
In the bunker	1 pt
Two or more shots in a bunker	2 pts
Out of a bunker into another	3 pts
Three or more putts	2 pts
Tee-off out of order	1 pt

The Scramble

This is a teams event with teams consisting of three or four players. On each hole each team member tees off and then team members choose which was the best drive. Each team member places their ball within one club length of the best drive, then plays their second shot. After all players have played their second shot, team members choose the best and all players play the next from that spot. Play continues in this fashion until the ball is holed. The Stroke score for the team's best ball is scored for each hole and the winning team (lowest score for 18 holes) for the day receives the prize.

There is one proviso: each player in each team must use their drive on at least three occasions.

Rotating Partners

This game is played in pairs with partners being decided by the toss of a coin. After six holes, players change partners and after 12 holes, players change partners again. For example, in a group of players A,B,C and D, if A and B initially play C and D, after six holes A and C play B and D and after 12 holes A and D play B and C. The wager is usually 50 cents or $1 per player per hole and the net best score for each pair wins the hole.

At the end of the round, players pool the 50 cents or $1 per player per hole and the pool is divided up according to how many holes each player won in the various pairs combinations.